Association American Art

Valuable Modern Paintings, Important Bronzes, etc.,

Collected by the Late William B. Bement

Association American Art

Valuable Modern Paintings, Important Bronzes, etc., Collected by the Late William B. Bement

ISBN/EAN: 9783744677325

Printed in Europe, USA, Canada, Australia, Japan

Cover: Foto ©Thomas Meinert / pixelio.de

More available books at **www.hansebooks.com**

CATALOGUE

OF

VALUABLE

MODERN PAINTINGS

IMPORTANT BRONZES, ETC.

COLLECTED BY THE LATE

WILLIAM B. BEMENT

PHILADELPHIA

FOR MANY YEARS A DIRECTOR OF THE PENNSYLVANIA ACADEMY OF THE FINE ARTS

TO BE SOLD AT ABSOLUTE PUBLIC SALE

ON MONDAY AND TUESDAY EVENINGS

FEBRUARY 27TH AND 28TH, AT 8 O'CLOCK

AT CHICKERING HALL

FIFTH AVENUE AND EIGHTEENTH STREET

ON FREE VIEW, DAY AND EVENING

FROM FEBRUARY 22ND (WASHINGTON'S BIRTHDAY) UNTIL DAY OF SALE, INCLUSIVE
(SUNDAY EXCEPTED)

AT THE AMERICAN ART GALLERIES

MADISON SQUARE SOUTH

THOMAS E. KIRBY   THE AMERICAN ART ASSOCIATION
AUCTIONEER   MANAGERS

NEW YORK
1899

CONDITIONS OF SALE.

1. The highest Bidder to be the Buyer, and if any dispute arise between two or more Bidders, the Lot so in dispute shall be immediately put up again and re-sold.

2. The Purchasers to give their names and addresses, and to pay down a cash deposit, or the whole of the Purchase-money, *if required*, in default of which the Lot or Lots so purchased to be immediately put up again and re-sold.

3. The Lots to be taken away at the Buyer's Expense and Risk *upon the conclusion of the Sale*, and the remainder of the Purchase-money to be absolutely paid, or otherwise settled for to the satisfaction of the Auctioneer, on or before delivery ; in default of which the undersigned will not hold themselves responsible if the Lots be lost, stolen, damaged, or destroyed, but they will be left at the sole risk of the Purchaser.

4. *The sale of any Article is not to be set aside on account of any error in the description, or imperfection. All articles are exposed for Public Exhibition one or more days, and are sold just as they are, without recourse.*

5. To prevent inaccuracy in delivery and inconvenience in the settlement of the Purchases, no Lot can, on any account, be removed during the Sale.

6. Upon failure to comply with the above conditions, the money deposited in part payment shall be forfeited; all Lots uncleared within one day from conclusion of Sale shall be re-sold by public or private Sale, without further notice, and the deficiency (if any) attending such re-sale shall be made good by the defaulter at this Sale, together with all charges attending the same. This Condition is without prejudice to the right of the Auctioneer to enforce the contract made at this Sale, without such re-sale, if he thinks fit.

THE AMERICAN ART ASSOCIATION,

MANAGERS.

THOMAS E. KIRBY, *Auctioneer.*

ARTISTS REPRESENTED

CATALOGUE

FIRST NIGHT'S SALE

MONDAY, FEBRUARY 27TH, AT 8 O'CLOCK

AT CHICKERING HALL

G. Bernheim
70. -

I

AUGUST SEIGERT   Dusseldorf
Reading the News

Although chiefly known and renowned for his large historical canvases, we still find Seigert devoting himself oftentimes to such small
cabinet pieces as we have now before us. This perfect type of a Bavarian
peasant, keenly studying the news of the day, with all the solid comfort
of pipe and beer, is full of interest.

Signed at the upper right.   Height, 10 inches; width, 8½ inches.

2

65. -

C. VAN WYNGAERDT   Antwerp
The Forest

m. R.
Snyder.

This wood interior is reminiscent of some of the best work by Diaz,
or the tall beeches surrounding the clearing might, from their force of

character, have been painted by Dupré. The puddle of water in the foreground mirrors beautifully the trees, while the old woman gathering fagots adds that note of humanity which makes nature doubly charming. This is a picture full of tone or quality, the colors vibrating through the whole in well-sustained gradations.

Signed at the right.   Height, 12 inches; width, 9½ inches.

3

C. M. WEBB   Dusseldorf

Old Woman Knitting

Old age will often work, because it is used to it, and could not bear idleness. The contented smile on this woman's face shows that her labor is light. Also in this example of Webb we find that grasp of character which signalizes the student of human nature, and that careful study of detail, without obtrusiveness, which marks the skilful craftsman.

Signed at the upper left.   Height, 11 inches; width, 9 inches.

4

V. CAPOBIANCHI   Rome

In the Park

Light and air are well depicted in this pleasant little picture. The two ladies have paused at the massive sculptured garden seat, such as were placed in gardens in the time when statues dotted the lawns and peeked through the branches of the groves. They nod together as blithely as the sunlight and the flowers about them. Technically the work has been done in delicate touches, with but little positive color, except in the flowers and in the dresses of the ladies.

Signed at the left.   Height, 7½ inches; width, 4½ inches.

VICTOR CHAVET   France

The Musical Amateur

The genre of this Member of the Legion of Honor is always satisfactory by reason of its well-bred suggestiveness and careful execution.
The animated concern with which the amateur is playing his bass viol is
well expressed.   The details of the composition are skilfully carried
out and show the influence of Roqueplan, who was Chavet's teacher.

Signed at the right.   Height, 9 inches; width, 7 inches.

JEAN MAXIME CLAUDE   France

Hunting Dogs

These dogs in leash are awaiting the hunter's coming.   They are
well drawn, and stand in the shady woods ready for the game.   The
wood interior itself is excellent.   The play of light, the bark of the
moss-touched white beeches, the cool atmosphere, make this an excep-
tionally strong hunting scene.   The artist is famed for these subjects,
and has received a number of medals for his various contributions to
European exhibitions.

Signed on the tree in the upper left. Dated, 1865.

Height, 9½ inches; width, 12 inches.

CESARE DETTI   Italy

Gathering Flowers

This talented Roman, whose studio at the present is in Paris, delights
in picturing rich costumes and colorful scenes.   His method and manner of doing this show the expert knowledge of a well-trained hand.
In this example the cold blue is dexterously handled with most pleasing
contrasts ; the patch of sky over the wall is luminous, and the shadowed
places heighten the effect of this charming picture.

Signed at the left.   Height, 9¾ inches; width, 6 inches.

van THEODORE FRÈRE   France

Halt in the Desert

This artist was the forerunner of many who have put the glowing
East on their canvas.   The first in discovery, he was not the least in
translating these Oriental scenes pictorially.   His many productions have
been eagerly taken up, a large number being engraved and reproduced
by other methods.   Ruskin, who was an enthusiastic admirer of his
talent, was the means of introducing him to the English market, where
he became exceedingly popular.   In fact, wherever his pictures have
been shown they have commanded merited prizes.

The picture shows us a soft and glowing crimson of sunset pervading
the desert air.   The caravan has halted on the edge of an oasis and
various preparations are being made for the evening meal.   Soon the
muezzin will call, and on the prayer rugs the evening prayer will be
chanted.   It is a typical scene of Oriental life, skilfully presented.

Signed at the right.   Height, 9 inches ; width, 13½ inches.

9

SALVATOR ALY   Paris

The Discharged Page

A picture to which imagination may put its own story.   Take away
the title, and how we could weave a tale of romance about the mandolin
on the low settee, the nosegay on the floor, and the book of poems on
the table.   The haughty bearing of the master may hide jealousy of a
wife's devotion, or a daughter's affection ; most probably the latter.

The minute execution, doing justice to every detail, to texture and
lighting, show a dexterous hand and sure brush.

Signed at the left.   Height, 9 inches ; width, 13 inches.

ROLAND BAUDUIN — Brussels

Ida

The Zingara of the Opera Masquerade, a gypsy of romance, with
large and dreamy eyes that tell of intense life, with well-poised neck and
womanly charms that ravish the eye of those that love the darker types.

Signed at the upper left. Dated, 1881, Height, 9 inches ; width, 7 inches.

LOUIS GEORGES BRILLOUIN — France

The Musical Enthusiast

The many medals which Brillouin received vouch for his popularity,
founded on remarkable merit. The whole is a well-executed *morceau.*
The old fellow's complete absorption in his music is shown by his stoop-
ing attitude in the tilted chair whereon he sits astraddle. Wig and
night cap are awry, and his eyes, his ears, his soul are centred in the
notes before him. His only audience is a dog, who is endeavoring to
sing to his master's fiddling, with results that may be imagined.

Signed at the right. Height, 10 inches ; width, 8 inches,

J. GUITEREZ — Italy

Italian Peasants

(Water Color)

Full of color, with a pleasant landscape setting. Body color is used,
giving a solid impression. The composition is far from the mereticious-
ness which often characterizes the later Italian school.

Signed at the right. Dated, 1869. Height, 14 inches ; width, 10 inches.

13

J. JULIANA   Rome

Trying the Finger-ring

(Water Color)

13 ꝰ

J. L. Warner

This picture is an excellent example of what may be accomplished with the subtle water color medium. The values of the white gown in its various folds are exquisitely given. There is no flatness about this interior, all the shades of the different planes are well given, and the textures cleverly suggested.

Signed at the right.   Height, 12 inches; width, 8¼ inches.

14

P. LINDER   Paris

Unmasked

¾. -

m. R. Snyder.

(Water Color)

The rounded form and piquant face, the airy gauze dress, and the coquettish toss of the head make a dainty picture. The lady is apparently ready for some flirtatious badinage.

The solidity of painting is caused by the use of body color in the white dress, which with its free and dashing handling makes this an exquisite example.

Signed at the right.   Height, 16 inches; width, 10 inches.

15

LOUIS LELOIR   Paris

Playing the Samisen

60. -

C. Blumenstiel

(Water Color)

A Parisian to the core, Leloir showed a most ingenious talent in color and in composition. His later style was not unlike that of Meissonier. His brilliancy was as evident in water colors as in oils.

The lady in this charming picture is a dainty Frenchwoman, posing in Japanese costume with Oriental surroundings, picking at the strings of a Japanese samisen.

Signed at the right. Dated, 1872.   Height, 9¾ inches; width, 13¼ inches.

LOUIS EUGÈNE LAMBERT   Paris

200. —

Adler Schwartz & fied

Kittens

Lambert and Madame Ronner are the greatest cat-painters of the day. The Frenchman is slightly ahead of his Belgian rival in popularity. His careful painting of humorous conceits in cat-life is thoroughly appreciated by those who desire a pleasing subject, combined with artistic excellence. As a pupil of Delacroix, Lambert has borrowed much of the richness of his master's palette, while his individual conception places him at the top of the limners of the feline race. The playful gambols of these kittens form a delightful study.

Signed at the right.   Height, 10¼ inches; width, 13¾ inches.

WILLIAM HART   United States

65. —

N. A. Price

Cattle

A native of Paisley, Scotland, William Hart was taken to America in early youth, and became one of our leading cattle painters. He is self taught and was elected a National Academician in 1858. This excellent example is one of his smaller easel pictures.

Signed at the left. Dated, 1871.   Height, 10 inches; width, 8 inches.

HERMANN HERZOG   United States

40. —

E. P. Anderson

Atlantic City Inlet

Fleeing from the approaching storm the fishing smack, under reefed sail, is scudding along for the safe harbor ; a man on the broken pier ready to lend a hand with coil of rope, if need be. The water is given in its true turbulent state ; the sky is dark and stormy.

Signed at the left. Dated, 1871.   Height, 13½ inches; width, 19½ inches.

FRIEDRICH KRAUS — Germany

The Garden Stroll

,3√. -

Roland. This genre and portrait painter was during the later part of his life one of the most popular members of the artistic colony in Berlin. Standing amid the dark-green foliage and flowers of her garden, this woman, with sunlight flickering over her white dress and making portions of it shine with soft, silvery tints, is a most attractive figure. The attitude is graceful, the composition simple, and the color refined.

Signed at the upper left.   Height, 21 inches; width, 13 inches.

C. E. PIERCE — United States

Cow and Calf

1 40. -

Avery

In a forest clearing cow and calf stand with bovine serenity bathing in the sunlight, which makes patches of brightness as it steals through the heavy, umbrageous trees. The drawing is excellent with charming tone and clear, clean color.

Signed at the right.   Height, 17 inches; width, 14 inches.

ANTON SEITZ — Germany

Roving Musicians

0 70. -

Took

This is a representative example of the best products of the Munich school. The microscopic brush work does not suffer the picture to fall into weakness. The details hold so well together, and the color is so skilfully graded, that with all its academic flavor the canvas is a most striking one. The light, centring around the nursing mother, is subtly gradated to the further corners.

The group represents a band of strolling minstrels, or mountebanks, who have been given shelter in a stable and are preparing their evening meal. The advent of viands is awaited with philosophic calm but pleasurable expectancy by the dog and the monkey as well as by their masters.

Signed at the right.   Dated, 1881.   Height, 11 inches; width, 16½ inches.

22

ALFRED STEVENS   Paris

In Memoriam

60
Roland.

Born in Brussels. This artist, after his studies in Paris were accomplished, acquired great fame with his graceful representations of elegant modern interiors enlivened with women's and children's figures. He became a master painter of beautiful women. The expression on the face of this devoted daughter betrays pent-up emotion while affixing the sprig of evergreen to the mother's picture. It is one of those pictures which, on account of its tender sentiment, it is well to live with. The voluminous black gown is well contrasted with the bright-colored chintz chaircover.

Signed at the right.   Height, 13½ inches; width, 10 inches.

23

GEORGE H. BOUGHTON   London

The Skipper's Watch

110.
G. Bernheim

George H. Boughton, taken early to this country, and receiving his training in Albany and New York, can scarcely be counted as an American artist. He has resided now for over thirty-five years in his native England, and although he often chooses for his subjects the Puritan Girl, as she is described in Hawthorne's tales, he still follows in methods the lines of the present English school. The subject before us is a typical English scene. The white chalk cliffs, the walled coast-guard station, and other accessories form a good setting for the group of "Age and Youth" in the foreground. The contrast between the weather-beaten old salt and the chubby little grandchild is well marked. The little ones playing on the old cannon, and the lookouts watching the ships in the offing, are secondary notes of interest.

Signed at the right. Dated, 1874. Height, 14 inches; width, 10 inches.

24

ALBERT BIERSTADT United States

10. -

Sunset in the Tuolumne—California

G. Bernheim Bierstadt was born in Dusseldorf, and was brought by his parents, in earliest infancy, to America, where they settled in New Bedford, Mass. After studying in Europe, he made a sketching tour of the Rockies and gathered there the material for his best pictures, such as "Mount Hood," "Estes Park," "Yosemite Valley," and "Rocky Mountains," which are widely known and have sold for very large prices.

In this easel picture, we find the moist air of evening charged with a hot, yellow glare of sunset, falling over the marshy meadows and edging the trunks of the big trees with lines of light. Deer are grazing on the rich grass of the bottom lands. The picture is more serious and subdued in tone than most of the artist's larger productions, which are sometimes rather spectacular.

Signed at the right. Height, 14 inches; width, 19¾ inches.

25

MARTIN RICO Spain

A View from the Garden

This is probably one of the best pictures Rico ever painted. It is the corner of a white mansion on the canal, similar to many in Venice, but it is so picturesquely presented that it takes the eye with admiration when the beautiful details are discovered. Nothing is slighted ; all is clear and true. The color of the sky, through which filmy clouds are travelling, vibrates in the shadows of this fine specimen of Rico's art.

Signed at the left. Height, 15 inches; width, 7 inches.

G. BOLDINI   Paris

300.
Kueeder.

. Song of the Bird

Boldini is well known in this country through his portraits of well-
known people and his charming small figure pictures. His style somewhat resembles Fortuny's, yet has an individuality of its own. His
brush is freer, his stroke more rapid. The lady, in summer costume
rambling through the tangle of high grasses and bristling bushes, is
graceful and captivating. The attitude well expresses her listening to
the song bird in the branches. The flecky clouds in the deep blue sky
add to the effect of the composition, which gives a charming ensemble.

Signed at the left. Dated, 1872.   Height, 21½ inches; width, 13 inches.

J. G. VIBERT   Paris

600 —
G. Bernheim

The Sleeping Sexton

Of all French painters the wittiest, and of *Boulevardiers* the most
charming, Vibert is popular in France even more than abroad. The
old saying of a prophet being without honor in his own country does
not hold true in his case. Medals and orders have come to him in
large numbers. The secret of this success? Vibert has always been
able to lift a page of human life, and that appeals to humanity. And
when a little spice in humorous satire is introduced, it is human to
enjoy a little teasing, especially if some one else is the object. Thus,
his slightly irreverent poking fun at ecclesiastics, not by any means
generally respected in France, has given him a hold on all classes.

It must be said that the artist, perhaps through the exigencies of
trade, is not always true to the highest requirements of the art which
he serves. The example before us presents him, however, at his best.
Who does not remember the pomposity of the French beadle? All will
then enjoy the man of straw in the gorgeous livery of this sleeping
Sexton. To touch on the other figures introduced : the fine irony,
and perfect appreciation of character can readily be recognized. The
execution, the technical perfection of this painting is, however, one of
its strongest points, for there is a fidelity, combined with freedom,
which makes this panel a perfect gem.

Signed at the right. Dated, 1871.   Height, 17¼ inches; width, 13 inches.

28

PAUL VERNON   Paris

5 y r°
J. H. Weimers

The Canine Pets

It is, perhaps, to be regretted that this artist, whose dexterity with the brush must remain unquestioned, seeks in his subjects and compositions almost exclusively to imitate his master Diaz. It almost seems as if the same models have served for both master and pupil; and as to color, as if the same palette were used.

It cannot, however, be denied that the dexterous handling of his implements has produced a most charming and colorful picture full of grace and sentiment.

Signed at the left.   Height, 17½ inches; width, 14½ inches.

29

R. DE MADRAZO   Paris

530.
Oehme

Languor: A Reverie

Raimundo de Madrazo, born in Rome of Spanish extraction (his father being the famous Madrid painter), and living in Paris, with frequent visits to New York, is a cosmopolitan by inclination, Parisian in spirit, and Spanish in verve and color. He needs no introduction to art lovers here, who have admired his life-like portraits of superfine appearance.

Indulging in the luxurious idleness of Cleopatra, this Spanish coquette, with bright eyes and sparkling smile, has her head filled with the fancies of her conquests. If any of her admirers should approach they would be ravished by her nonchalance and charm.

The picture is exquisitely painted with sure touch and delicate handling of the effect of light.

Signed at the left.   Height, 17 inches; width, 21½ inches.

ADRIEN MOREAU   Paris

Rambling—Springtime

M. R. Snyder

70.

Moreau paints many pictures of life in the French courts of the last
two centuries, in a spirited and humorous manner, which are well-known
here by reproductions. He lives, however, also in the present, as Ma-
demoiselle Frou-Frou before us will suggest. It is a delicate Parisian
fancy, this ramble in the fields in the dainty costume of pleasing colors.
The clump of bushes and bank of verdure serve as a good setting to
the figure. The manner of handling the distance with its placid river
and hills beyond shows that technical skill for which the artist is celebrated.

Signed at the right.   Dated, 1872,   Height, 21 inches; width, 17½ inches.

GUSTAVE DE JONGHE   Belgium

Hide and Seek

80. —

R. Ho. Loor

The scene is pretty ; the child dragging *Polichinelle* by his string is
cunning ; the woman an image of motherly happiness—thus far the subject. Technically the work is equally interesting. The relief of the
black dress against the screen should be noticed. There is excellent
drawing. The room is full of light, life, and atmosphere.

Signed at the left.   Height, 21¼ inches; width, 17½ inches.

HEINRICH HANSEN   Denmark   *125. —*

The Armory

Chas. O'Reilly.

Born at Hadersleben, and a pupil of the Copenhagen Academy,
Hansen soon became noted for his correct architectural drawing in his
genre painting. He broadened his scope by his travels through Ger-

many, Western Europe, and Spain ; while the honors which gradually came to him culminated in his appointment as professor at the Copenhagen Academy.

The Armorial Hall represented in this picture is a most interesting example. The bright sunlight plays and sparkles over the steel armor and polished surfaces of the marble columns which support the vaulted roof. The various workmen engaged in repairing the baronial trappings are interrupted by the Master's approach, who is descending the curious, spiral staircase leading from the upper hall. There is a wealth of antiquarian study suggested in this composition, which, together with the well-defined execution, makes it an unusually attractive painting.

Signed at the lower right.   Height, 17½ inches; width, 22½ inches.

33

BIANCHINI   Italy

Madame Le Brun

This is a portrait of Madame Le Brun in her younger years, by an Italian artist, who took the features from one of the many self portraits of this famous Frenchwoman.

Height, 22½ inches; width, 16 inches.

34

LADISLAUS BAKALOWICZ   Poland

The Morning Call

A scene at Warsaw, with the grandames exchanging courtesies in the aristocratic mansion. The rich interior, with marble columns at the entrance, and solid buffet at the side, are a worthy setting to the sumptuously rich costumes of caller and hostess. A beautiful picture in which the skill of showing of texture must be remarked in the blue velvet robe, and the rich white satin dress with creamy lace.

Signed at the left.   Height, 21½ inches; width, 16 inches.

35

B. C. KOEKKOEK   Holland

Landscape

M. Finlay *200.*

Barend Cornelis Koekkoek was a painter who had cut loose from
academic methods in a time when such action was an unpardonable
heresy.   He painted nature with care and smoothness, yet with the
nervous energy of a man who is strong in his brush and palette.   He
may be considered to have been the Dutch complement of the French
so-called Barbizon school.

His first training was received from his father, a noted marine
painter, but he soon became a pupil of the Amsterdam Academy
under Schelfhout and Van Os.   In 1841 he travelled in Belgium, the
Ardennes, and along the Rhine.   Later he founded an academy in
Cleves.

The landscape before us is from his later period, showing the landscape of one of the Rhine tributaries.   It has all the points of excellence
by which Koekkoek became famous.

Signed at the right.   Dated, 1852.   Height, 17½ inches; width, 22 inches.

36

WILLIAM M. HARNETT   United States

From Bohemia

170.- *Adler Schrang & Fischel*

This is one of those aggregations of objects which must have been
found in some fourth floor studio of the Quartier Latin.   Study the
various implements which make up this still-life, and you can picture
to your mind's eye the long-haired, bespectacled owner of all these ingre-
dients of good cheer.

The painting is very clever; marble slab, copper jug, parchment book,
pipe and tobacco all showing true to nature.

Signed at the left.   Dated, 1888.   Height, 21½ inches; width, 25½ inches.

PETRUS VAN SCHENDEL   Belgium

Market by Candlelight

80.

A. Steckler.

This pupil of the Antwerp Academy is the most famous painter of such candlelight effects as we have now before us. He was the first to successfully give those peculiar light notes produced by various sources, not strong in themselves. Many have since essayed to solve this most difficult problem, which also "the little masters" of the Flemish school loved to experiment on. Van Schendel's work is deservedly found in most of the European museums. This picture is painted with the smooth finish of the pupils of Baron Wappers, so unlike the broader touch of the Dutch school. Although there are various light sources in this picture, there is no conflict, each being well kept to its proper strength ; the light centre puts the two main figures in delicate relief.

Signed at the right. Dated, 1866. Height, 25 inches ; width, 19¼ inches.

FLORENT WILLEMS   Paris

Good News

120.-

E. P. Bar...

Born at Liège, Willems studied especially the Old Masters, after his talents had shown themselves during his apprenticeship with a picture restorer. When but seventeen years old he attracted great attention, and his first picture was hung in the Salon when the artist had barely turned twenty-one. Such precocity, however, did not end in a fruitless after life, for the name of "the Belgian Meissonier" which has been given him, attests the rapid progress which Willems has made in his art.

His minuteness of detail in this picture is combined with ease of handling the colors, which are subdued and rich ; the textures are given with wonderful fidelity, the heavy portière in the background being especially correct. There is a deftness in the handling of the shadows which denotes a master in chiaroscuro. The values both of the dark and the light gowns should be noticed.

Signed at the right. Height, 28½ inches ; width, 23 inches.

J. G. BROWN United States

The Passing Show

A man forced to do a thing he likes, is doubly happy. This is the case with J. G. Brown and his bootblacks. His work is very popular. The canvas here shows five street urchins, and shows them perhaps better than the later well-known youngsters with which we are so familiar. The tone of the picture is better than that of some of the artist's later work. The expression of expectancy according to the characters of these boys, is inimitable.

Signed at the right. Dated, 1877. Height, 19½ inches; width, 29½ inches.

L. COMELERAN Paris

Twilight Landscape

"Twilight gray
Had in her sober livery all things clad,
Silence accompanied."

This is the subdued sentiment of this exquisite canvas. There is no *tour de force*, no specious trickery of golden bars of clamorous hue, so common in an evening twilight. The landscape is bathed in the soft, rich light which has deep shadows as its foil.

This Parisian artist is of a serious bent of mind, as is readily seen in this work. He loves to picture the rural road, the suburban dwelling, the rustic scene, rather than the gay surroundings of his town studio.

Signed at the right. Dated, 1872. Height, 20 inches; width, 27½ inches.

R. S. DUNNING United States

Apples and Straw Hat

An admirable piece of still life. The apples are most naturally painted, while the color is rich and resonant.

Signed at the left. Height, 19 inches; width, 25 inches.

42

IGNACE DE LÉON Y ESCOSURA　　Spain

Sans Invitation

Born at Oviedo, this artist became a pupil of Gérôme in Paris. His natural bent is towards historical research, the results of which he introduces in the genre pictures which he mostly paints. He is not a stranger in this country, which he has several times visited to paint local subjects and portraits.

The story told by the picture before us is, in spite of its irreverence, an amusing one. The devil-may-care swashbucklers are making themselves thoroughly at home in a place where the latch string surely did not hang out for such as they. The mock servility of the carbineer in the hall-way proves that the smile on the face of the poor monk pouring the wine is but *bon mien au mauvais jeu.*

The details of composition should be studied—the poses are so natural and easy. The values are skilfully handled. It is a charming picture.

Signed at the left. Dated, 1871.　　Height, 19 inches; width, 23½ inches.

43

BLAISE ALEXANDRE DESGOFFE　　Paris

Objets d'Art in the Louvre

Desgoffe, who paints exclusively still life, has brought. himself to marvellous perfection in this branch of art, and may be considered without a rival; this place of eminence being assigned him by no less a judge than Hamerton, the famous English critic. It is known that his dexterity in skilfully imitating on canvas costly works of art has procured him access to the treasures of the Louvre, a privilege granted to no other artist.

The picture before us is a marvel of dexterous representation. The crystal vase is transparent as its original; the ivory mug with silver mountings shows the same rich sheen and delicate carving—there is, a curious little figure of St. George; the onyx goblet, the loose flowers carelessly thrown among these precious articles, the rich embroidery of the heavy tablecover, each is represented with microscopic minuteness, yet with realistic force.

Signed at the left. Dated, 1868.　　Height, 24 inches; width, 21 inches.

44

RUDOLPH ERNST   Germany

Moslems at Prayer

The muezzin has sounded the call to prayer from the minaret, and
these Mussulmans perform the devotions of their faith. With out-
stretched hands the one, the other in squatting posture, yet both devout.
The beautiful temple interior, the textures, the rich coloring, the loving
touch of a not too hasty brush, all combine to make this a desirable and
satisfactory painting.

The elaborate and appropriate frame is in harmony with the picture.

Signed at the left. Dated, 1885.   Height, 25 inches ; width, 20½ inches.

45

A. F. BUNNER   United States

Ponte Vecchio, Venice

Andrew Fisher Bunner was born in New York. For five years he
travelled through Germany, France, and Italy, in which latter country
he was especially attracted by picturesque Venice. He remained there
several years, his views of that wonderful city being so highly prized
that he scarcely had time for the delineation of other subjects.

Signed at the right.   Height, 21½ inches ; width, 31½ inches.

46

JOSÉ VILLEGAS   Spain

Wayside Discussion

Heat and light were never more powerfully represented than on this
canvas, for the sun seems fairly to rain light upon the white walls and
the blinding sand. The greatest skill is required to paint a work like
this, for if clear whites are used the effect is chalky and the sense of heat
is lost, while if the highest notes of color are adulterated or neutralized

to an appreciable degree, the vividness is gone and the sense of light is lost. In this picture the technical methods for mingling white with sunlight have been used to perfection. The scant vegetation of spiked bushes and hardy cacti indigent to African soil are truthfully given, while human life in all that torrid heat is presented in the idling, gossipping Moors, the approaching horseman in the middle distance, and the listening woman over the wall. It is an African scene of wonderful power and vividness.

Signed at the right.   Height, 21 inches; width, 31½ inches.

47

WILLIAM T. RICHARDS   United States

Conanicut Island

(Water Color)

William Trost Richards is a native of Philadelphia, a pupil of Paul Weber, a German artist of that city. He travelled extensively through Europe. His excellent work procured him an Honorary Membership to the National Academy of Design.

This scene presents a rocky cove on the shore; a party of tourists have just returned from a stroll on the island and are yet lingering in this romantic spot. A well-painted composition.

Signed at the right. Dated, 1881.   Height, 22½ inches; width, 36 inches.

48

THOMAS HILL   United States

Pond Brook, New Hampshire

Born in Birmingham, England, this artist came to America when about twelve years of age. He is mostly self-taught, and has had studios in Boston, San Francisco, and Philadelphia. His California scenery is quite popular, while at the same time he has looked for quieter

24

effects with equal success. In this picture there is a charming summer day depicted, in the trout season, the artist himself whipping the stream for speckled beauties. Tender light filters through the summer foliage, and the brook, reflecting both sky and leaves, shows tints of blue and green, of sapphire and beryl. The gnarled oaks and leafy maples edge the clear water, in which the bright pebbles are visible. It is a summer idyl.

Signed at the right. Dated, 1874. Height, 29¼ inches; width, 24½ inches.

49

KLOMBECK AND VERBOECKHOVEN Brussels

Landscape and Sheep

The early Dutch and Flemish schools are especially rich in examples where artists combined their specialties to produce a picture of more than ordinary excellence. Rubens often painted the figures in the landscapes of some of his friends, while Breughel and De Mompers likewise produced such dual works. The combination in this case is a peculiarly happy one. Verboeckhoven's *forte* is sheep, while the landscapes of Klombeck, with their heavy, unbrageous trees, are regarded as being far above the common. There is great depth and distance in this canvas, there is the fresh coolness of the morning air, the babbling brook, and the quiet motion of the journeying flock—all that which makes the landscape perfect.

Signed at the left. Height, 23½ inches; width, 34 inches.

50

ANDREAS ACHENBACH Germany

After the Storm

This strong and vigorous naturalistic painter may be considered the least addicted to the mannerism of the Dusseldorf school, to which by early instruction and later affiliation he is considered to belong, and of which he is by far the most distinguished member. His early views of the Rhine, fresh and individual, indicated already the breadth and vigorous grasp with which he was to treat mountain, forest, and the sea alike, after his travels through Holland, Norway, the Bavarian Tyrol, and Italy.

The heavy clouds, the wind-shaken trees, the muddy road, relieved by the struggling sun-ray breaking on the white cottage wall, make this picture a most characteristic example. The people who have sought shelter under the hospitable roof, picturesque with its dormered window, have emerged and are wending their way homeward, some still lagging behind at the door. These people, however, only add life to the scene. The strength of the canvas lies in the broad treatment of rock and tree and elements at war. It is one of those pictures which gave Achenbach his wide celebrity, and for which he was awarded numerous medals and various honors.

Signed at the left.   Length, 30 inches ; width, 21 inches.

51

DON LUIZ ALVAREZ   Spain

Preparing for the Masquerade

This contemporary artist, a pupil of the elder Madrazo, was born in Spain, and studied some years in Rome. His first picture, painted in Florence in 1861, though completed in the face of depressing difficulties, obtained a medal, and when taken to Madrid, excited such favorable comment that the way to substantial success became easy. His style, somewhat florid, is ever full of contrast, his composition well contrived and attractive.

The story of this painting is well told. The centre of attraction is the youth, who is being prepared to masquerade as a lady. The gown is held up for his inspection, dainty fingers arrange his coiffure, while witty hints as to his behavior are given him by his masked vis-à-vis. The secondary group, flirting at the mirror, the peeper around the screen, the worrying spaniel, the garniture of the chamber are all skilfully arranged and most effective.

Signed at the right. Dated, Roma, 1871. Height, 23¼ inches; width, 31 inches.

JOSEPH COOMANS Belgium
A Basket of Flowers

E. Brandus.

This widely-travelled artist, who was born in Brussels, was first instructed in Ghent by Hasselaere, himself but a mediocre artist, and later at the Antwerp Academy by de Keyzer and Baron Wappers. He went with the French army to Algiers, where he spent several years, then visited Italy, Turkey, Greece, and the Crimea. Returning to Italy in 1857, he was attracted by the Pompeian paintings and subsequently painted almost exclusively subjects from antiquity. He had a studio in New York in 1889–90.

The Roman lady before us, holding the basket of flowers, is an ideal beauty. Her white skin, blonde hair, glossed by sunbeams, graceful robes draping the well-drawn figure, and rich ornaments, form a most attractive picture of refinement and breeding.

Signed at the left.   Height, 31¾ inches; width, 25¾ inches.

53

ALEXANDRE CABANEL Paris
The Evening Star

Cabanel was born at Montpellier. His earliest work was devoted to historical genre and portraiture. Previous to 1861 he painted in the classical style of David, of which no trace is visible in his later work. He was a master of the human figure and exemplifies in many of his nudes the contention that the female form divine is the idealization of beauty, the artistic enjoyment overcoming sensuous suggestion. Besides being the recipient of many honors, not the least of which was the *Grand Prix*, he also held a professorship in the *École des Beaux Arts*.

The delicate, chaste rendering of this floating figure bearing the evening star is most charming and full of spiritual sentiment. The filmy drapery does not hide the graceful lines, nor can the ease of arms and half-turned head be well improved upon. The whole suffused in that pale bluish light which a rising moon imparts adds a dreamy softness to this poem of the night.

Signed at the left. Dated, 1875.   Height, 36 inches; width, 20¾ inches.

54

EUGÈNE VERBOECKHOVEN   Belgium

Sheep in the Stable

1570.

E Wesden

No man has ever been able to give the woolly texture of the sheep coat like Verboeckhoven. Whatever foundation there may be for criticism on his placing animals against the sky, it is beyond cavil that his barn interiors are the best of his work. The rich light falling through the open door in this stable is excellently used for the play of values, which are well sustained. This is a most representative example of the artist's best manner.

Signed at the right. Dated, 1867.   Height, 29 inches; width, 39¾ inches.

55

DON VINCENTE PALMAROLI   Spain

Selling Antiquities

1550.

Beel j'a.

Palmaroli is one of the chief painters of his school. In color and style he somewhat resembles Fortuny, being slightly more reserved and subdued. The picture before us is the most important specimen of his work in this country. There is the effusive richness of a Moorish bazaar in the wares littered about and held up for sale. The Señoritas in their picturesque costume, the señor hidalgo with his señora, the burnoosed Moor on the metal-mounted chest, and the antiquary are portraits from life. The color is full and opulent, and the texture-painting perfect.

Signed at the right.   Height, 27 inches; width 35½ inches.

56

LUDWIG MEIXNER   Germany

The Moon on the Waters

140

M. N. York.

This Munich artist excels in moonlight scenes, to paint which he was inspired after some visits to Norway and Sweden, wherewith he completed his study years. In this picture the full radiance of the northern moon is shown as it falls from behind the filmy clouds upon the waters. There is a well-thought-out effect produced by the dark silhouette of the graceful bark against the sky. The dimly seen headland, and the boat pushed out into the rippling surf, which just catches a few light-rays, combine to produce a composition enhancing the masterly light effect.

Signed at the left. Dated, 1872.　　　Height, 45 inches; width, 34 inches.

57

FRIEDRICH KRAUS　　　　Germany

The Necklace

160

W. M. Loor.

This picture is painted after the best manner of the German artists, with softness and simplicity of coloring. Though subdued, the tone is rich, and in the morbidezza may be found something of that ripe, luminous, ideal quality of color which is often found in the nudes of Rubens; this picture rightly lacking the voluptuous fulness of the models of the great Flemish painter. The string of pearls, exquisitely painted, gives title to the picture. It is a most attractive face, a graceful pose, and has an excellent foundation in the heavy red cloak.

Signed at the right.　　　Height, 30½ inches; width, 25½ inches.

58

HERMAN TEN KATE　　　　Holland

Headquarters of the Guard

170.-

C. C. Anderson

This eminent Dutch artist, whose works since his death have greatly enhanced in value, was born in The Hague, and became a pupil of Kruseman, at Amsterdam. He early distinguished himself, winning a medal when but nineteen years of age. The patriotic love of Hollanders is the cause of the avidity wherewith this artist's historical works are being collected for preservation in the various provincial museums of Netherland.

The panel before us shows an incident at the end of the sixteenth century in the great eighty years' war of Holland with Spain. A lieutenant has brought a message to the Senior and Junior Captains of the troop, who are discussing the reply to be made. The tri-color in the corner, the oldest national flag used at the present day, had just been adopted as the ensign of victory. The coloring is beautifully harmonious, the grouping picturesque. It is one of those story-telling pictures which do not lose by this quality, as here it does not detract from the artistic and suggestive excellence.

Signed at the right. Dated, 1868.   Length, 25 inches; width, 37½ inches.

59
RICHARD BURNIER   Germany
Cattle

Burnier was born in Holland, but was early taken to Dusseldorf. After his studies there, he elected to follow more the promptings of nature, schooling himself also in a study of the Dutch masters. Although taught at one time by Achenbach and Schirmer, he left their style completely, preferring after his visit to Paris to follow Troyon and the French idyllic painters. The example before us must at once be recognized as the work of one whose conception of art was broad and vigorous. These cows are vital and real. Few painters outside of the Dutch school, however, have so well put atmosphere on their canvas as Burnier has succeeded in doing here. It is the heavy morning dew, through which the farmer with his milkpail yoke is seen approaching. This is an example worthy of the best cattle painters.

Signed at the right. Dated, 1876.   Height, 24¼ inches; width, 34 inches.

60
CORELLI   Italy
The Old Witch

A picture somewhat lurid in color, for which an old Italian woman furnished an expressive model. The weird surroundings of snakes and lizards and the bright lights furnish a picturesque ensemble.

Signed at the right.   Height, 40 inches; width, 26½ inches.

J. CAROLUS   United States

The Chess Players

An excellent subject picture in which the expressive countenance of each person shows absorption or interest. The costumes are gracefully depicted. A picture of refined elegance well executed.

Signed at the left. Dated, Bruxelles, 1872. Height, 32 inches; width, 41 inches.

ALBERT F. BELLOWS   United States

Into the Sea

Bellows was chiefly known for his water colors, although his oils are of special importance. This is a charming subject of the elder sister giving the younger one her first ocean dip. The color is pleasing, with further good points in sky and water.

Signed at the left.   Height, 41½ inches; width, 33¾ inches.

HENRY BACON   America

Paying the Scot

Henry Bacon, who has an honorable record as a veteran of the war of the Rebellion, serving with distinction in a Massachusetts regiment, has attained distinction with his cleverly contrived scenes of village life.

In this picture a travelling artist dashes a fresh coat of paint on the inn-keeper's old sign-board in payment for his reckoning. Of course he attracts almost the whole neighborhood, whose various poses and actions are given with telling strokes. Special attention should be given to the smoker sitting at the window on the left.

Signed at the left. Dated, 1870.   Height, 34 inches; width, 45 inches.

64

EDWIN LORD WEEKS   United States

The Three Princesses in the Alhambra

The three Princesses here represented were the daughters of Moham-
med the Left-Handed—Zayda, Zorayda, and Zorahayda—whose story
is told in Irving's "Alhambra." The first two eloped with Christian
lovers, through fear of whom their father had confined them in this
tower.

This interior gives an idea of the splendor of the Alhambra in the
days of the Moorish occupancy of Spain. The minute carvings and
arabesques, the green and gray tessellations in the pavement, the lavish
color on the walls, the bright rugs, costumes and metal-work, illustrate
the fertility of the Oriental fancy. Weeks, like Bridgman, is a pupil of
Gérôme, and like him, paints few except Oriental subjects.

Signed at the right.   Height, 31 inches ; width, 39 inches.

65

EDWARD H. MAY   United States

The Song

A most serious problem, happily solved. It required a bold and
daring artist to portray a woman in the act of singing. In this case the
attempt was crowned with success. The pose is graceful, the tilt of the
head expressive, the texture of the dress excellent, and there is a
splendid background to it all. The early training of this artist by
Daniel Huntington in New York, and Couture in Paris, is manifested
in the surety of handling of this subject.

Signed at the left. Dated, 1880.   Height, 45 inches ; width, 29 inches.

66

PIERRE AUGUSTE COT   Paris

The Coming Storm

The artist, a native of Bédarieux in southern France, was a pupil of
Cogniet, Cabanel, and of Bouguereau. His individual style shows yet

32

the excellences of each of these masters. He wedded a daughter of Durlet, who designed the caryatids that surround Napoleon's tomb. Being almost exclusively a painter of portraits, his work is little known outside of France, though all his canvases are pictures of great worth. He was one of the decorators of the Hôtel-de-Ville, destroyed by the Commune.

There is a curious conflict of title in connection with this picture. It has always been known as "The Coming Storm," whereas in Europe the reproductions, which are amongst the most popular known, are called "Paul et Virginie" from the love-idyl of Bernardin de Saint-Pierre. This picture antedates by a few years the larger replica, which now hangs in the Metropolitan Museum. It is a most captivating production. The lithesome swarthy youth, the lovely maid in diaphanous robe of white, the play of light on the musing figures, the threatening darkness forked by lightning—all is presented in masterly fashion, full of grace and tender feeling.

Signed at the left.   Height, 47 inches ; width, 31 inches.

67

ADOLPH SCHREYER   Germany

Siberian Travellers

Adolph Schreyer was born in Frankfort-on-Main, in affluent circumstances, which enabled him, after coming to years of discretion, when a life choice was to be made, and he found the artistic fire burning within him, to give himself, without care, to a thorough training for his profession. He was attracted mostly by the horse, and he studied "man's best friend" in the riding-school and anatomically. When, in 1848, he travelled with his friend, Prince Turn und Taxis, through Hungaria, Wallachia, and Southern Russia, he laid the foundations for that almost exhaustless series of bold and dashing subjects for which he has become world-famed. His later travels, in 1856, through Syria and Egypt, brought forth the ripe and rich reflections of the artist's colorful mind in those Arabian horsemen which have fierce force yet subtle poetry. If a distinction is, however, to be drawn, we will find greater sincerity in his early period—more concession to the demands

33

of trade, hence lack of thoroughness and inspiration, in the Arabian period.

In this picture there is no need to point out that mull, soft, knee-deep snow, the gusty cold wind, the sere leaves on the bramble-bushes, the fine values of white on the snow—all go to make an exceptional picture by a famous painter.

Signed at the left.   Height, 29 inches ; width, 55 inches.

68

LÉON PERRAULT   Paris

The Fisher Girl

Perrault was a pupil of Picot and Bouguereau, and learned from them the scrupulous care with which he finishes his figures. Sometimes he indulges his fancy in the portrayal of gay dames in high life, at other times he is more seriously inclined. Then he invests the types of lowly life with pathos and poetry, and teaches lessons of deeper import, while showing the patience and gentleness of these children of the poor.

In this picture he shows a face, such as we sometimes meet in the highways and byways of labor—earnest, sincere, melancholy even, yet gentle and loving. Of the technique we need only to remark how wide the color scale, yet how harmoniously arranged. The atmosphere is good, while a beautiful sky bends over the sea.

Signed at the right. Dated, 1870.   Height, 55 inches ; width, 37¾ inches.

69

H. BOLTON JONES   United States

Tangiers

Scarcely an exhibition passes that the work of this artist is not seen. Lately, however, there have not as important works come from his hands as the one before us. It is a splendidly executed canvas, in which many technical difficulties have been successfully overcome. The city on the hill, with its clay, gleaming walls, the green native growth, and the desert cacti, are all faithfully shown in their true values and planes. The touch of deep-blue sea in the far-off distance adds a coolness to the color scheme which is particularly happy.

Signed at the left. Dated, Tangier, 1880. Height, 36 inches; width, 53½ in.

70

HERRMANN HERZOG   United States

Niagara by Moonlight

Herzog was born in Bremen, and after his studies in Dusseldorf were completed, he travelled extensively through Norway, Switzerland, Italy, and the Pyrenees, in which countries he painted numerous mountain landscapes, which are excellent in drawing and pleasing in color. In 1869 he came to America and settled in Philadelphia, where he soon became a prominent member of the guild of the brush. His wide travels in this country produced some of the best local scenery ever painted. "Niagara by Moonlight" must be noted for its reserve. There is little of the lantern slide about this picture. It is simple, and through its simplicity as fascinating as that mightly thunderous roar of the "King of Waters," the pride of this continent.

Signed at the left. Dated, 1872.   Height, 55 inches; width, 46¾ inches.

71

LOUIS MOUCHOT   France

Sortie of the Grand Council

Of the artist: He was born in Paris, paints genre and landscape, dipped his brush in Egyptian sunlight, while schooling himself to portray nature in truth, thus he earned medals and the Legion of Honor.

Of the picture: It is a grand work, nobly done. "The Stones of Venice" never were brought together in simpler truthfulness to the bold sweep of the façade of the palace. The architectural detail, the linear and aërial perspective, are a fit framework for the exquisite marshalling of the various groups which now attract our attention. The Doge just descended to the foot of the staircase is surrounded by courtiers and counsellors, many following, others preceding. How each face shows character. Dignity, diplomacy, cunning, intrigue, pride, are all depicted in these portraits, one might call them for their excellence. Then admire the reserve of color, where the temptation for garish brilliancy would be great. It is a beautifully toned picture of admirable strength.

Signed at the right. Dated, 1872.   Height, 46 inches ; length, 70 inches.

72

WILLIAM T. RICHARDS   United States

Marine

" Thou glorious mirror, where the Almighty's form
    Glasses itself in tempests ; in all time,
Calm or convulsed—in breeze, or gale, or storm,
    Icing the pole, or in the torrid clime
Dark-heaving—boundless, endless, and sublime—
    The image of Eternity—the throne
Of the Invisible ; even from out thy slime
    The monsters of the deep are made ; each zone
Obeys thee ; thou goest forth, dread, fathomless, alone."
                                        —BYRON.

Signed at the left. Dated, 1883.   Height, 39½ inches ; width, 72 inches.

first evening $21.640.-

SECOND NIGHT'S SALE

TUESDAY, FEBRUARY 28TH, AT 8 O'CLOCK

AT CHICKERING HALL

73

AUGUST SEIGERT   Dusseldorf

P. Parsons 80.

Threading the Needle

A characteristic example of one of the foremost men of the Dusseldorf School. The details are carried out to perfection, while yet the
great interest centred in finding that eyelet adds so much zest to the
picture. It is without doubt a clever bit of painting.

Signed at the upper right.   Height, 10 inches; width, 8½ inches.

74

DAVID COL   Belgium

J. J. Gibbs 290.—

The Sportsman's Rest

David Col was born in Antwerp and became a pupil of the Academy
in his native place under De Keyzer. His pictures, which are mostly
on a small scale, are carefully executed, without excess of detail, and
are found in nearly all the museums and private collections of Belgium.
This genre is an excellent specimen of his usual work, with those little
touches here and there which make a picture real. The painting of the
various still-life parts should especially be noticed.

Signed at the right. Dated, 1873.   Height, 11½ inches; width, 9½ inches.

37

75

J. JULIANA   Rome

At the Bull Fight

(Water Color)

40. -
R. a
Smith

A Spanish scene of the national sport. The toreador, burly-looking,
stands on the raised circle surrounding the arena, ready to jump in the
ring when the opportunity comes to deal the fatal thrust. The specta-
tors back of him are enthused by the spectacle. There is good color in
this suggestive scene.

Signed at the right.   Height, 12 inches; width, 8 inches.

·

76

HUGHES MERLE   Paris

Mother and Child

105. -
E
Karanaugf

The artist was a native of St. Marcellin, became a pupil of Cogniet,
and for a time painted life-sized pictures of subjects taken from the life
of the poor. Later he devoted himself to more cheerful compositions.
The little picture before us can from internal evidence be assigned to
the best period of the master, about 1870. The color tone is rich yet
soft, with accurate drawing and poetic feeling.

Signed at the left.   Height, 8¼ inches; width, 6¼ inches.

77

C. P. REAM   United States

Still Life

45. -
J. cl. Gibbs.

The grapes have the gloss of the luscious tokay, the peaches the
velvety down of our California product, the rosin pearl which like a
tear drop hangs to the blushing cheek is transparent, the wine glass,
likewise beautifully painted.

Signed at the right.   Height, 9¾ inches; width, 11½ inches.

78

FRANZ ITTENBACH
St. Catherine

Germany

110. —

J. E. Bright

Ittenbach was born near Cologne, and received his early training in
Dusseldorf, but allied himself with the Munich school, in which place
he chose his residence. He painted historical subjects, portraits, and
some famous frescoes in the churches at Remages and Neuss. He was
a close student of the Florentine masters, taking from them his ornate
color and decorative motives. The circular panel of St. Catherine is
indeed "a picture of silver in a frame of gold." The angelic expression
of the face belongs to the saint who listens to the heavenly choirs. The
jewels of the dress and crown add richness and splendor to the whole.

Signed at the left. Dated, 1872.   Circular, 12 inches diameter.

79

H. SINKEL
Inspiration

Dusseldorf

85. —

J. B. Walker

Henricus Johannes Sinkel was born in Almeloo, Holland, and became a pupil of Karl Muller at Dusseldorf, in whose style he paints
religious subjects and portraits. His touch is subtle, his lines are fine,
his color rich. This idealization of the painter's art, lifting the soulful
eyes to the inspiring vision, is a splendidly composed symbolism; the
painter could no better prove his conception of the spiritual side of
his art.

Signed at the left. Dated, 1871.   Circle, diameter 5 inches.

80

RONALD BAUDUIN
Clara

Brussels

85. —

C. Weston

An ideal head, showing a charming profile, a cascade of golden hair
rippling over the pearly shoulders, and a gossamer veil encircling the
well-poised vignette. The whole is relieved against a rich background
of intense blue.

Signed at the upper right. Dated, 1881.   Height, 9 inches; width, 7 inches.

C. M. WEBB   Dusseldorf

Old Man Smoking

100.-

C. Weston

There is much latent humor in this character study. The old fisherman, with his wise friend sitting on his hand, is evidently luxuriating in
the sweet hour of rest. The type is perfect; the rugged features, in
which toil has plowed many furrows, are full of expression. The accessories, where textures are shown, manifest a careful and well-schooled
hand. The artist builds his work on the lines of the Dusseldorf school
with the inspiration of the old Dutch masters.

Signed at the left. Dated, 1865.   Height, 11 inches; width, 9 inches.

82

FIRMIN GIRARD   Paris

The Picnic

130.-

C. A

Kavanaugh

Girard is a genre painter, whose fresh and brightly colored pictures
of everyday life are well liked. There is a good deal of sprightliness
about the various persons scattered here in this sylvan grove, where the
brook babbles over the smooth rocks. The costumes of the day were
always given by Girard with minute care and an eye to picturesque dis-
play. The blue parasol makes a cool note in this shady glen, well
expressing the pleasant enjoyment in this secluded spot, when out on
the dusty road the sun must be uncomfortably beating down, when it is
able to send such a strong ray on the central figure.

Signed at the left. Dated, 1876.   Height, 9½ inches; width, 13¾ inches.

83

J. R. GOUBIE   Paris

The Favorite

460.

Randolph

eyebi

Jean Richard Goubie was born in Paris. He became a pupil of
Gérôme, from whom he took that exactness of drawing which we admire
in his animal subjects. Whether painting a falcon hunt or a ride on
the seashore, his style is always spirited and his subjects interesting.

Here we can readily understand the care this horseman has for the fine-bred hunter, which with his own hands he leads to the pasture, as he takes down the bars of the gate. This is a noble animal with spirit and gentleness. The landscape is delightful.

Signed at the left. Dated, 1886.   Height, 9 inches; width, 12 inches.

84

HERMANN HERZOG   Paris

Head of the Saco River

Those who have journeyed among the White Mountains will recognize this scene at a glance. The little lake is the one near the head of White Mountain Notch, wherein the Saco takes its rise. The river flows through the craggy portals seen beyond it and winds about the foot of Mount Webster, whose huge bulk constitutes what is known from this position as Elephant's Head, which looms up through sheeted rays of sunlight and lords it over the landscape. This scene of solitude and sublimity is well reproduced on the canvas, where the full grandeur of the deep cañon is visible before us.

Signed at the left. Dated, 1871.   Height, 13½ inches; width, 19½ inches.

85

CAV. ATTILIO SIMONETTI   Italy

The Meeting

(Water Color)

As a pupil of Fortuny, Simonetti imbibed the glowing love for color of his master; his work is noted for its brilliancy, yet strengthened by a judicious use of heavier shades. A professorship at Naples attests the esteem in which he is held by his countrymen.

The three beauties on their afternoon ramble meet a gallant, who readily would have foregone this triple pleasure for a single meeting. Still, he is ready in his merry mood to pass, " like coin, the tinsel click of compliment." The rich dresses in the dark setting of foliage fit well on images of delicacy and grace.

Signed at the left. Dated, Roma, 1873. Height, 15 inches; width, 19¼ inches.

86

G. FERRARI   Italy
The Suspicious Coin

110.

Fo Nieter

As professor of the academy at Bologna, his native place, Giulio Cesare Ferrari has exercised great influence on the later Italian school. As may be seen in this picture, this influence can only have been for the best, for the vivid colors, so natural to the painter of sunny Italy, are subdued and modulated. This cabaret interior is most picturesque, and the posing of the figures is artistically conceived.

Signed at the right. Dated, Roma, 1872. Height, 18 inches; width, 14½ in.

87

MARTIN J. HEADE   United States
Vase with Flowers

65.

C.
Karanaugh

Martin J. Heade was born in Bucks County, Pa. After a sojourn of two years in Italy, where he studied in the various museums, he went to South America to gather sketches of the fauna and flora of Brazil. These sketches, originally intended for a book on South American humming-birds, are now owned by Sir Morton Peto, London. In all his work there is manifest a decided love for color, as is shown in this loosely arranged vase of flowers, which is charming for its delicate tints; while the rich and heavy curtain on the right forms an effective foil.

Signed at the right.   Height, 16½ inches; width, 13 inches.

88

C. HARRY LATAN   England
English Landscape

35.

& J
Barnes

A characteristic view. In the foreground a field with daisies; houses loom up behind the trees. An agreeable subject of restful quiet, with delightful color; well-executed composition.

Signed at the right.   Height, 13 inches; width, 16½ inches.

42

J. GUITEREZ   Italy

Alone

(Water Color)

25. —

X. E. Bricort

An Italian peasant woman, belonging to the well-to-do class, stands
in meditation in the woodland clearing.   This is a good study, in which
the picturesque local costume is given with much fidelity.

Signed at the right,   Height, 14 inches; width, 10 inches.

LUCIUS ROSSI   Paris

" The Priestly Monitor "

170. —

@. Kavanaugh

A *précieuse* with her duenna, instructed by the Carmelite brother on
the vanities of this world—with what success we leave open for specula-
tion.   The florid and ornamental style with purity of color make this
decorative panel exquisite and dainty.   The tapestry painting on the
rear wall of the open summer-house is well produced, the head and
hand of the preacher are perhaps the finest points in this picture.   Rossi,
a Frenchified Italian, is well known by the fac-similes in color of his
works which occasionally come from Paris.

Signed at the right,   Height, 18 inches; width, 15¼ inches.

GUSTAVO SIMONI   Italy

Market Scene in Naples

(Water Color)

130. —

E. Weston

Oriental subjects attract this Roman colorist.   He gives them with
force in the presentation of character, with a ready grasp of local color
and a keen eye for passing incident.   Bright summer sunlight is here

bathing the white walls of a Neapolitan street, where all is bustle and confusion. There is a happy mingling of buyers and sellers, donkeys and *paniers*, cabbages and ropes of onions, a bewildering array, skilfully put together without jarring contrasts of color. It is a cleverly painted picture of attractive quality and direct method.

Signed at the left. Dated, Naples, 1880. Height, 13 inches; width, 20 inches.

92

F. VENIA   Florence

The New Vintage

An extremely high finish has been put upon this picture, for the artist has painted it with affection and enjoyment. The ripening wine that gleams in the trooper's glass has been served to him from the wicker-covered bottle. The girl who holds this bottle, and who leans against the huge barrel, looks up at him piquantly, laughing at his critical air, for your soldier is usually glad enough to get his wine anyhow, and is not scrupulous as to the quality if the quantity suffice. The figures are wrought against a background of shadow that fills a dark and cavernous cellar. The representation of substance and texture is remarkable in its finish and minuteness.

Signed at the left. Dated, 1875. Height, 15¼ inches; width, 19¼ inches.

93

GIUSEPPE CASTIGLIONE   Italy

Expectancy

Arrested action is excellently given in this pose of the young girl who on her way in descending the stairs stops on the landing to look out of the window in the thick castle wall. The view *to her* may not be assuring, for the rain-sodden landscape and muddy road may not hasten the coming of the expected one. *To us*, however, that glimpse in the mountain valley is most delicious, for there is the moist atmosphere, the breadth of rolling hillside, waving pines, all contained in

that framework of battered plaster and shrunken wood jambs. We
must not neglect, however, to turn again to the figure to admire the
daring combination of red bodice and light-green skirt; the scheme is
most successfully carried out, without obtrusion to the eye, and is, on the
whole, very pleasing. The artist is always happy in the presentation
of youth and beauty.

Signed at the right. Height, 18½ inches; width, 12 inches.

94

ORESTE CORTAZZO Paris

Taking Leave

The scene is from Napoleon's time. The red hussar uniform of Mu-
rat's cavalry fits picturesquely on the well-built young lieutenant; the
lady in the case, estranged or only piqued for the present, is attired in
the long-trained silken gown of the period. We need not search further
into the merits of the story—a romance after all depends on the point
of view. The excellencies of execution here are, however, more to
our favor; and the ready brush and steady hand are easily recognized
in the assurance wherewith the various textures are given; the carpet,
the Persian rug, the brass stand for the palm—they all vie with each
other to show the skill of this Italian artist who has made his home in
Paris now for a number of years, meeting with great success in his
artistic productions.

Signed at the left. Height, 17½ inches; width, 12¼ inches.

95

F. DVORAK France

Portrait

(Pastel)

A most charming, refined head, with blonde hair; a large bunch of
violets resting against the white dress.

Signed at the left. Dated, 1898. Height, 27 inches; width, 17½ inches.

MARTIN RICO   Spain

On the Cornice Road

6 ̄ ʃ. —
p eʀ·· e

A child of nature, with no other studio but creation's temple until
he had won recognition, Rico reproduces on his canvas the tenderest
and most delicate moods of brilliant skies, and houses and trees quiver-
ing in the sunlight. Born in Madrid, he had some instruction from the
elder Madrazo, but winning the *Prix-de-Rome* he went to Paris, where
he was greatly aided by Zamacoïs, Meissonier, and Daubigny.   When
looking at his pictures do we not find there some of the best peculiarities
of each one of these men?   There is a gray tone running through the
picture before us, which is full of radiance, widely differing from some
of his intenser color schemes.   It is the slumberous quiver of warm,
sweet air, slightly veiling the houses and trees in the middle distance,
and throwing a delicious atmospheric haze over the mountains far away.
The water in the foreground, placid as a mirror, reflects its borders in
a cooling manner ; while the shade of the little grove invites the group
under one of the trees to the *dolce far niente* of the Italian noontime.

Signed at the right.   Height, 15 inches ; width, 37¼ inches.

97

WILLIAM H. LIPPINCOTT   United States

Picking Flowers

(Water Color)

40. —
P. ʃr
(ʀ aꞈꞈ·

This New York artist, born in Philadelphia, has steadily advanced
in his art, and has become a favorite contributor to various exhibitions.
The summery landscape before us is a pleasing and natural composition,
showing the enjoyment of city folks when "the town, made by man,"
is left with all its oppressive house fronts, and "the country, made by
God," opens its welcome.   The terrier enjoys the pleasant surroundings.

Signed at the right.   Height, 16 inches ; width, 13 inches.

PAUL VIRY   France

The Engagement Ring

The daintiest conceit—one thinks of the little spyglass of a kodak, where nature is put in miniature, with exactness of line. The utmost refinement and grace mark this charming panel picture. There is nothing lacking to augur the utmost happiness for the pair that in this trysting-place now pledge their troth. The picture is painted with great delicacy, in a key of light and silvery color.

Signed at the left. Dated, 1874.   Height, 11½ inches; width, 13½ inches.

EDUARDO ZAMACOÏS   Spain

The Old Gardener

The short life of this gifted Spaniard was the romance of the *Quartier Latin*. He combined the satire of Goya with the wit of a Frenchman, and preached his pictorial homilies with the precision of his master, Meissonier. He was a master of the grotesque at will, but appreciating more fully the picturesque, he was a mocker without a grimace. He was brilliant without false glitter ; audacious in his invention, yet disarming, because the point of his arrow was not poisoned. "The Education of a Prince," of the Salon of 1870, a satire keen and scathing, was his masterpiece—and his swan song. This little easel picture gives splendid proof of the fine technique of our artist. It is a thorough character study.

Signed at the centre.   Height, 11 inches ; width, 8 inches.

THÉODORE ROUSSEAU   France

Landscape

No artist ever delved deeper in the profound mysteries of nature than Rousseau. The grand aspect of the landscape and its tenderness were equally familiar to him. He rendered with the same mastery the smile of creation and its terrors. In the great forest of Fontainebleau, with its mossy trees, that have outlived the eagle, he drew his inspiration from the eternal source of beauty. Ofttimes we

> " See the fading many colour'd woods,
> Shade deep'ning over shade, the country round
> In brown ; crowded umbrage, dusk and dun
> Of every hue, from wan declining green
> To sooty dark."

In this charming landscape we see the rocky hillside and clump of trees submerged with superb light, while the peasant, resting by the wayside, adds a delicate touch of poetry.

Signed at the left.   Height, 8½ inches ; width, 10½ inches.

101

ALBERT LAMBRON   France

Seeking Knowledge

Albert Lambron des Piltières, which is his full name, was born at Saint Calais. As a pupil of Flandrin, he selected historical and genre subjects sometimes verging on the bizarre, but always showing great talent and humor combined with technical skill. This little cabinet shows us an *Incroyable* of the First Empire, enjoying a shady nook and a few pages of his scientific treatise, in preference to a practical pursuit after botanical and entomological treasures. A few flowers at his side on the bench are ready for the herbarium at his feet, while the net is ready to hand to capture the butterflies which soon will be found among the shrubs and flowers. A most charming composition, executed in a thoroughly satisfactory manner.

Signed at the left. Dated, 1873.   Height, 5½ inches ; width, 4 inches.

102

W. S. COLEMAN   England

Joyous Days

Coleman's work is much sought after for reproduction, as it combines grace and beauty. This child driving a shuttlecock, with tiger skin around the waist, is like the dainty setting of Tadema's Roman Atrium. It is a fine bit of painting in a very attractive style.

Signed at the left.   Height, 19 inches ; width, 14 inches.

48

V. DUVAL
Paris

Gallery of the Louvre

160.--

Any one who has visited the "Treasure House of France" will be astounded at the photographic exactness of this picture. Yet not photographic, as the perspective is drawn according to the visual, not the lens, focus. The fresco decorations of the ceiling, the elaborate finish of the walls, the wonderful exactitude of the cabinets in the centre with their wealth of jewels and *orfèvrerie*—all make this a most valuable reminiscence of European travel.

Signed at the right.   Height, 16½ inches; width, 24 inches.

AUGUST LEU
Germany

Scene in Northern Italy

180.

This landscape painter, who was born in Münster, and received his education there, was one of the few artists who have been able to give mountain scenery with breadth and vigor, yet with simplicity. His travels in Norway and Switzerland instilled in him this love for mountain vastnesses. In this picture he presents one of the sapphire sheets that nestle in the Southern Alps. The picturesque crags and wooded borders around the placid water, the peasants in their rural pursuits, the clear atmosphere, with lazy clouds sailing along, are all suffused with fine mellow color.

Signed at the left. Dated, 1872.   Height, 31 inches; width, 43 inches.

100.--

E. M. A. ANDRÉ
France

The Duel

A typical French subject. The peculiar poplars, the high, shorn hedge, the peaked roof of the house hidden beyond, the last century garments of the principals and their friends, all bespeak the usual surroundings of *une affaire d'honneur*. The grouping is skilful and illustrates well the story ; the early morning air is well shown in the beautiful sky and atmospheric impression. It is one of those decorative pictures which is pleasing in spite of its gruesome subject—but then, it is a French duel, and, perhaps, not so gruesome after all.

Signed at the left.   Height, 23 inches ; width, 19 inches.

106

HENRY FARRER   United States

Fisherman's Home

(Water Color)

Henry Farrer is, perhaps, best known by his etchings, but his pictures are equally good. This fisherman's cottage on the coast stands in high relief against the cloudy sky. Rocks and trees protect it from the stormy blast. The clear air, coming night, and vast stretch of ocean, are well expressed.

Signed at the left. Dated, 1880.   Height, 16¼ inches ; width, 27½ inches.

107

KRUSEMAN VAN ELTEN   United States

Landscape

(Water Color)

This artist, at present residing in Paris, is a constant and valued contributor to the various exhibitions held in New York and Philadelphia. As a native of Holland he has inherited the intuitive and sympathetic feeling for the charming moods of nature which he produces with great success in all his works.

Signed at the left.   Height, 23½ inches ; width, 17½ inches.

JEAN BAPTISTE ROBIE   Belgium

Flowers

This is a capital example of rare quality of this modern master in the field of still life. The exquisite delicacy and fulness of this painting breathes, as it were, the perfume of "the children of summer." The silver tankard is rendered in masterly fashion. Robie has received many medals and decorations in recognition of his superior talent. His works are found in many private collections. This example was purchased from the Belgian Exposition, held at the Pennsylvania Academy of the Fine Arts, Philadelphia, 1882.

Signed at the left.   Height, 24 inches ; width, 18 inches.

ALBERTO PASINI   Italy

Market Scene in Asia Minor

Born near Parma, Pasini has that eye for color which marks his countrymen. In his study years in Paris he had several masters, taking from each that which he was best qualified to receive—from Ciceri his drawing, from Isabey color, and from Rousseau that sentiment which oftentimes spiritualizes the whole. No man succeeds better in realizing upon canvas the splendor, color, and brilliancy of burning light, or the barbaric sumptuousness of gorgeous pageantry. His well-schooled hand has a broad touch, yet is not negligent of detail. His light effects are often peculiar and always striking. The color of this market scene 'is rich, not glaring—rather subdued, a skilful symphony of the chromatic scale. The animated groups of mingling Cossacks and Turks are naturally disposed. The picture is one of the best examples that ever left Pasini's easel.

Signed at the right.   Dated, 1881.   Height, 21 inches ; width, 25¼ inches.

EDWARD MORAN   United States
Homeward Bound

Edward is one of the prominent members of a numerous artist-family. He unites here his specialties of marine and figure painting. His figures remind us of those of Perrault and Jules Breton, and commonly illustrate the life of fisher-families on the French coast. The figures in the distance are well painted; those in the foreground full of movement. The color scheme is good, with a fine sky.

Signed at the left.   Height, 25½ inches; width, 17¾ inches.

CHAS. LINFORD   United States
Landscape

'' A fine sky overarches this charming landscape, with clumps of trees in the middle distance, and cattle standing in the shade. Beyond, is a line of trees with cottages.

Signed at the left. Dated, 1888.   Height, 18 inches; length, 26 inches.

H. HAGER   United States
The Baronial Hall

This is a remarkably fine piece of relief painting, showing the exquisite carving of the solid oak wall panels. The light through the window, which creeps along the polished floor, is cleverly handled and distributed. The chandelier is exquisitely finished. This picture shows a fine brush handled with skill and discrimination.

Signed at the right.   Height, 22½ inches; width, 28¾ inches.

113

MILNE RAMSAY   United States
Still Life

This Philadelphia artist had great success at the Paris exhibitions after his studies with Bonnat were completed. This picture is a bright, bold, manly piece of work, painted with little artifice, but with much genuine knowledge. The arrangement is simple and unconventional, and there is an admirable rendering of textures. The smooth glass and china, the nuts and fruits, the plush cloth—each seem to be painted with a different touch and to exhibit a different phase of the artist's technical versatility.

Signed at the right. Dated, 1872.   Height, 28½ inches; width, 23 inches.

114

P. VIGNERON   Paris
Watering the Wine

One of the tricks of the trade is here exposed, the artist having caught the portly wine merchant in the act of increasing his stock without the trouble of buying it. "Remember, my boy," said the dying wine merchant to his son, "that wine may be made from anything, even grapes." This gentleman is apparently one who indorses this statement, for he believes that it can be made from water. He is sampling the mixture in a businesslike way, and the assistant, who holds the bucket, casts a sly glance at him, as he pauses in the execution of this miracle of turning water into wine.

Signed at the left.   Height, 23½ inches; width, 28½ inches.

115

WILHELM KOLLER   Germany
The Parting

Born in Vienna, Koller became a pupil at the Academy of the Austrian capital, afterwards continuing his studies at Dusseldorf and Antwerp. After a brief sojourn in Brussels he returned to Germany. He

painted principally historical genre, of which the present work is
an excellent example. The care which Koller always uses in finishing
his work, without vexatious minuteness of detail, is well shown. The
play of sunlight outside the door where the soldier's farewell takes place,
is technically a fine bit of painting, the whites and yellows being
exquisitely modulated. The perspective through the door-arch is correct. The figures themselves are faultless, the bit of by-play of the
passing comrade, looking back, right in place. The principals express
in pose and action the shadow of the parting sorrow.

> " And to his eye
> There was but one beloved face on earth,
> And that was shining on him."

Yet they are sustained by the thought that welcome will smile again,

> " And farewell goes out sighing."

Signed at the left.   Height, 26¼ inches; width, 23¼ inches.

116

G. BAUGNIET   Paris

Interesting the Convalescent

The sick woman in this picture has been propped up on pillows in an
easy-chair, and a young friend or relative is posing before her in a new
dress, which a maid is adjusting. The faces are pretty and animated,
and the nun who attends the convalescent betrays by her sidelong
glance at the new dress, the fact that she is not wholly unconscious of
the vanities of the world she has forsworn. The group is clever in
arrangement and the picture pleasant in color.

Signed at the right. Dated, 1874.   Height, 24 inches; width, 27½ inches.

117

R. S. DUNNING   United States

Fruit-Piece

This Fall River artist has presented a rich and decorative canvas of
fruit admirably arranged in luscious profusion, and painted with sincere regard for form and color. The various fruits retain their own
softness or solidity, the accessories are faultlessly rendered.

Signed at the right. Dated, 1873.   Height, 29 inches; width, 24 inches.

118

J. G. BROWN   United States

"John Anderson My Jo"

6 75.

The President of the Water Color Society is a stranger to no one
who has but the slightest interest in art.   Yet here we find him back to
his earlier work, like his "'Longshore Men at the Noon Hour," which
was recently shown at a Lotos Club exhibition.   This picture is painted
in a broader and more vigorous manner than we now expect from his
hand ; and owing to the subject the picture is the better for it.   It is
a most characteristic old couple, breathing the sentiment of the famous
poem.   The subject of this picture will never be copied by the artist, as
attested by a letter from his own hand.

Signed at the left.   Height, 23½ inches; width, 29½ inches.

119

B. VAN MOER

Venice

2 25. —

Venice, "the Bride of the Adriatic," nowhere looks more entrancing
than at this spot, the entrance to the Grand Canal ; nor does she ever
look more serenely brilliant than in the late afternoon when the sun has
passed the meridian and is fast disappearing.   Then the deep blue of the
sky reflected in the quiet waters suffuses the whole with that luminosity
which only the Italian sky possesses.   The scene is animated by passing gondolas and sailboats.   The linear perspective is carried out with
consummate skill from the Custom House at the point to the stately
domes of the Santa Maria della Salute farther on, and so beyond to
the houses and palaces that line this main artery of the city of a hun-
dred isles.   The artist has given a remarkably inviting presentment of
this picturesque point of view.

Signed at the left.   Height, 17 inches; width, 30¼ inches.

CHARLES JACQUE France

Landscape with Sheep

Charles Émile Jacque was the last survivor of that era of artistic revolution in France which has influenced the art of the world. Early in life he was a map engraver and a soldier, and commenced drawing on wood and etching. By choice he became a painter of rustic life, with a predisposition to the humble animal side of it. His early experience as an engraver gave a firm and precise hand, whereby his drawing is absolutely faultless, while his vigorous strokes make his composition bold and decisive.

The sheep here shown, drinking at the pool, may be called one of the best painted flocks of the artist's favorite subject. The fine green of the grass and the rugged trees are to be noted.

Signed at the left. Height, 31 inches; width, 25 inches.

M. KING United States

Assets of a Poor Artist

A suggestive piece of still life with its dog-eared book, lump of bread, various other books, and seashell, well painted. The artist hails from Philadelphia.

Signed. Height, 29 inches; width, 27 inches.

F. P. MICHETTI Italy

Gathering the Flock

Francesco Paolo Michetti is one of the rising Italians, whose French training has toned down his national tendency to high colors. The silhouette-like figure of the picturesque girl, standing out clear against the evening sky, is most attractive; the landscape, the turkey flock, the river beyond, with the reflected sky, are all painted in a broad and free manner.

Signed at the right. Dated, 1871. Height, 20 inches; width, 31½ inches.

EMILE VAN MARCKE France

Cattle

Van Marcke was born in Sèvres, and early made his living as a por-
celain painter and decorator in the National Pottery. There he attracted
the attention of Troyon, at whose advice he studied from nature. At
first his diffident steps did not progress, but by dint of perseverance he
left his imitation of his friend and teacher and became the individual
master, who only can be compared as a cattle painter with Troyon,
Cuyp and Potter. His color is fresh, lively, more brilliant and sparkling than shown by his teacher. He was a master draughtsman, his
grouping is always pictorial, yet true. His landscapes possess an equal
degree of excellence and are replete with the charms of joyous nature.

In this remarkably beautiful picture one of the choicest examples of
this painter's art is shown. The very nature of the bovine race is por-
trayed in the vague look, the philosophic indolence of these shaggy
beauties. The fields have just been refreshed by a heavy shower, and
the cattle seem to enjoy the return of sunlight as it falls through the
breaking clouds. Yet the atmosphere is wet, and the dampness which
mingles with the sun's rays makes the air more luminous.

Signed at the left.   **Height, 26½ inches; width, 32½ inches.**

CONSTANT TROYON France

On a Branch of the Moselle

(Pastel)

Something in the very name of Troyon suggests gentleness and refinement. He was a poet, and gave a poetical interpretation of nature. His
was a largeness of life that found the tendrils of beauty where many
pass by its outward form unrecognized. With discriminating care to
portray in deep, pure colors what his soul felt, a nervous breath lies

trembling on the canvas which he has touched. Of his landscapes it may be said :

> " Here are cool mosses deep,
> And thro' the moss the ivies creep,
> And in the stream the long-leaved flowers weep,
> And from the craggy ledge the poppy hangs in sleep."

In this beautiful pastel we find the sky calm and serene, of ethereal blue ; the tender atmosphere, the glow of summer sunlight, the body of water still and unbroken, the peasants in commonplace pursuit—the whole a sublime landscape.

It might be in place to point out the absolute perfection of this picture, which for over twenty years was in Mr. Bement's possession. And yet there are those who think a pastel is too easily damaged ; while on the contrary in this point it stands on the same line with the other mediums. It is, however, softer, and may, perhaps, be handled with more poetic feeling than the water color.

Signed at the left.   Height, 25 inches ; width, 20 inches.

125

A. R. D. CROCHEPIERRE   Paris

Satisfaction

This picture was bought from the Paris Salon of 1888, and shows excellent handling of a sympathetic subject. The old woman holding the distaff is well painted, especially the face and hands, showing superior ability in the artist. The quaint French kerchief over the head and the woollen cloth have fine qualities of texture.

Signed at the right. Dated, 1887.   Height, 16 inches ; width, 12 inches.

126

A. EGUSQUIZA   Spain

She Laughs at His Folly

This light-minded pair, an idle dame of fashion and her foppish caller, illustrate a phase of life which is curious to us, without arousing our sympathy. Still there are interesting points about this sparkling bit of color. The grace and luxury of it all is apparent, the dexterous if perhaps daring use of certain colors in complement is highly successful, the Japanese decorated screen in the background adds the tone of solidity, and restores the balance of what otherwise might have been unduly gaudy.

Alberto Rogelio de Egusquiza, which is the artist's baptismal name, has achieved a deserved reputation in Madrid with like compositions. He is the painter of high social life *par excellence*.

Signed at the right.   Dated, 1873.   Height, 18 inches; width, 13½ inches.

127

PHILIPPE BENOIST   Paris
Napoleon's Tomb

This picture of a magnificent shrine (for such it now is), the Rotunda of the Invalides at Paris, is of historic and architectural interest. The people who have gathered here have uncovered their heads, for in the sarcophagus, guarded by sculptured angels and surrounded by the battle flags of France, sleeps—if that active and ambitious spirit can sleep—Napoleon Bonaparte, the man of destiny; the soldier who wielded a power unknown since the days of Alexander and Cæsar; the general whose armies' tread shook all Europe; the wondrous founder of an ignominious dynasty. The fine architecture of the building, the marbles, the tessellated floor, the fine light effect in one of the mortuary chambers are given *con amore*. It was a task which this well-known French artist approached with reverence and devotion.

Signed at the right.   Dated, 1863.   Height, 15½ inches; width, 12 inches.

128

THEODORE CERIEZ   Belgium
Talking Politics

This is a French inn with figures full of animation. The animated argument of the trio in the foreground will not disturb the good cheer of the worthies at their luncheon. The groups outdoors are occupied in the everyday manner of village life. The execution shows a following of careful, academic lines.

Signed at the right.   Height, 15 inches; width, 11 inches.

EDWARD NAVONNE   Paris

Approaching a Climax

55..

E. C.

Anderson

An exquisitely composed panel, with a well-executed decorative color scheme. The blue of the lady's robe is gracefully draped and finely painted. The cavalier' s costume is rich and picturesque, the furnishing of the chamber is in excellent keeping. Of course a question is being asked.

> "When love once pleads admission to our hearts
>   (In spite of all the virtue we can boast),
> The woman that deliberates is lost."

It is not likely that either will be disappointed, for where there is a willing ear, as here seems to be the case—the answer may be guessed.

Signed at the left. Dated, Roma,1872. Height, 13½ inches; width, 10¼ inches.

JOSÉ VILLEGAS   Spain

The Guard and His Dog

850.—

e. ñ

Primm...

This pupil of Fortuny, whose manner he followed to a certain extent, had for a time a studio in Rome, and is now settled in Paris. He has a thorough knowledge of the human figure, and a fine talent for composition. In execution he combines breadth of treatment with a close attention to detail, always appreciating what is essential and what should be passed lightly, so as not to detract from the main features. He possesses great skill as a colorist, sometimes being even more gorgeous than Fortuny ; his intense realism saving him from extravagance in this dangerous facility.

The guardsman with his pike-staff, in buff leather dress, with the magnificent deer-hound at his side, is a piece of solid and serious painting, full of character ; the curtain, splendidly executed, forms a fine background.

Signed at the right. Dated, 1875.   Height, 35 inches ; width, 23 inches.

WILLIAM T. RICHARDS United States

View in the Adirondacks—Autumn

185.

W. A. Price

Indian Summer, the most glorious and gorgeous time of all the year. A smart painter pictures then what he sees, a good painter subdues the loud and glaring colors, which on canvas would look garish. The long, slow ascent of forest-covered slopes is aglow, yet tempered with subtle atmosphere. The view is happily chosen, and the still lake adds beauty to wood and mountain.

Signed at the right.   Height, 24½ inches; width, 39½ inches.

A. BONIFAZI Italian

Carnival in Rome

110.-

Windmuller

With all the good natured hilarity of a Latin crowd, these peasants and city folks, mingle *rus in urbe*, in the carnival festivities under the shadow of the Colosseum and the Arch of Titus. There is no confusion in the clever grouping but a dexterous variety of occupations and movement. The whole is suffused with a rich twilight, fast passing into dusk while the moon is wheeling into the heavens.

Signed at the left. Dated, Rome, 1872. Height, 19¾ inches; width, 42 inches.

JAMES HAMILTON United States

Marine—Sunrise

105.-

E. A. Osborn

Hamilton was born in Ireland but early brought to this country. He studied, and after travelling settled in Philadelphia, where he became best known by his illustration of "Dr. Kane's Arctic Explorations" and other works. In his easel pictures he gave himself mostly to marine views and he delighted to depict the grand, often gloomy aspect of the ocean.

A bold headland is shown in this picture upon which a wreck is grounded. Behind it rises a mountain of sublime height and awful form. The sea is breaking in heavy surf upon the beach, while the gulls sailing over the waters announce the new storm coming. It is an impressive painting of the ocean in one of its wild and dangerous moods.

Signed at the left.   Height, 29½ inches; width, 49 inches.

134

KLOMBECK AND WILLEMS   Belgium

Winter Scene

2 05.
ø
Yaranaugh

Another painting of dual production, of which Klombeck has strongly furnished the landscape, in which Willems has introduced the figures. Each has contributed such excellent parts that the whole makes a superior painting. There is a chilly atmosphere, with the leaden sky overarching the skeleton arms of the denuded trees.

Signed at the left. Dated, 1866.   Height, 36 inches; width, 48½ inches.

135

Picking Cherries

2 500.
Eo.
Me Mullin

W. BOUGUEREAU   France

Bouguereau has latterly become identified with bisque-looking bathers and other model copies, with a classical execution of well-defined line, where all the world seems to have rushed into the naturalistic movement.

The Bouguereau of a score of years ago was more serious. He had then arrived at that perfect technical knowledge and masterly skill in handling his implements which puts him in the very front rank of the masters of his art. An exquisite example of this we find in this canvas, which is one of the truly artistic gems of the Bement Collection. The whole is conceived in a refined style, with that inimitable grace which makes even the peasant child an idyl. The delicate seriousness of the face, lit up by those wonderful blue eyes, with the flaxen hair as a halo, is perfectly captivating. There is no pose, no weariness of arrested action, but a natural movement in the uplifted arms, with the cherry just plucked. The summer air, the rich dark foliage, give an *envelope* to this picture which make it idealistic.

The romantic life of Bouguereau, his capturing a prize from the competing art students, while he himself was but a clerk ; his continuing triumphs ; his celibacy, because of his mother's objection to the woman of his choice ; his final marriage to her after twenty-five years' waiting —all this is well known. His artistic eminence in the school of his choice, and in the conception of art which he follows, is beyond' cavil.

Signed at the left. Dated, 1871. Height, 51 inches ; width, 34 inches.

136

CARL KUWASSEY, PÈRE   Austria

The Tyrol

Mountain scenery—the towering cliffs, the enveloping clouds, the dark mysteries of recessed cañons—how suggestive it is of the grandeur of creation. There is a theory that mountain scenery is of too vast extent ; that there is too much perspective in it ; that it becomes panoramic, and, therefore, does not answer to the simplicity of true landscape painting. In refutation of this we may point to the mountain scenery of Jacob Ruysdael among the Old Masters, or to the grand canvases, with swishing clouds, and breadth and immensity, which Courbet painted when in exile in Switzerland. Or, to come nearer home, who does not admire the mountain views which La Farge gives us ? Mountains are not beyond the artistic grasp. The canvas before us proves this contention. The artist, an Austrian by birth, although living mostly in Paris, began life, as did Munkácsy, as a carpenter, and always adhered, after his professional life had commenced, to the love for his beautiful Tyrol, as shown in his bold, strong, and airy canvases.

Signed at the left. Dated, 1872. Height, 50½ inches ; width, 37½ inches.

ALEXANDER A. LESREL   Poland

Meditation

4,25.-

E. Wreston Lesrel was born in Warsaw, where he received his first instructions, afterwards studying in Dresden and Munich. He settled in his native place, where he attained great popularity by painting scenes from Polish history. The genre before us indicates the versatility of this artist, as well as the careful presentation of his subject. Noticeable is the exquisite manner of painting the heavy embroidery on the dress, and the strings of pearls adorning this Polish beauty. The jewel casket on the table and the roses in her lap, divergent in texture, are given with equal facility. The light through the window, affording a good city perspective, fills the room. One can walk around the chair, which stands out clearly from the wall.

Signed at the right. Dated, 1882.   Height, 35 inches; width, 27¾ inches.

5,80.- ## HERMANN HERZOG   United States

Van Yockenburgh.

Lake George

The wild woods, rocky heights, and unkempt fields are shadowing in the gloom of an impending storm. The heavens are darkening, but a gleam of light pierces the clouds and falls across the foreground, where a pleasure party is speeding up the road in a carriage. The view is from near Caldwell, at the head of the lake, or southern end, the point whence the traveller first sees this exquisite sheet of water. The mountain landscape from this point is superb. The Fort William Henry Hotel is seen on the left, and one of the little steamers that ply on the lake is seen beyond it.

Signed at the right. Dated, 1872.   Height, 40¾ inches; width, 59 inches.

WILLIAM M. HARNETT   United States

On the Window Shutter

"The Old Barndoor" is a well-known picture which has been reproduced *ad nauseam*. The picture before us presents, with the same idea,
a more artistic ensemble. The musical instruments, hung up against
the old board window shutter, hang loose from the background, and are
remarkably vivid with all the *vraisemblance* of nature. The beautifully
carved frame adds to the setting of the picture.

Harnett was born in Philadelphia; was a pupil of the National
Academy, and studied also from 1880–1884 in Frankfort and Munich.
His work is well liked and readily purchased.

Signed at the left. Dated, 1889.   Height, 61 inches; width, 41½ inches.

EDOUARD RICHTER   France

In the Cathedral

Richter, of German descent, but born in Paris, has all the instinct of
the French School, showing his tutelage under Hébert and Bonnat in
his careful work. This is a picture, with huge, dim spaces, of the
famous Cathedral St. Gudulle at Brussels, lit by the prismatic brilliancy
of stained-glass windows, and relieved from heaviness by ornate Gothic
architecture and Renaissance ironwork. An air of religious quiet per-
vades the sanctuary. The woman who is leaving the church shows her
faith by her works in handing her alms to the needy.

Signed at the right. Dated, Bruxelles, 1871.

Height, 57 inches; width, 39 inches.

141

ORESTE CORTAZZO   Italy

Crowning the Bride

1400..
S. P.
Bayue

But few artists can compose a picture so well sustained in all its various parts as this one. With its many groups it is splendidly balanced, and the interest and animation of every figure perfectly sustained.

The picture presents a custom in France during the reign of " Le Grand Monarque." The royal standard waves in the presence of the king. A bridal pair will be honored because royalty happens to visit one of its many summer palaces, just when the wedding is to be celebrated, and the king will crown the bride of the day. The Dauphin sits on a rug on the balustrade at the right, an interested spectator, soon to look down, however, when the mortars go off, which the royal huntsmen are preparing. The opulence of color is subdued with rare judgment; yet showing the richness and brilliancy of the costumes of the times.

Signed at the left,   Height, 34 inches; width, 57 inches.

142

2 65.

LÉON OLIVIÉ   France

Van

Falstaff and Doll Tear-Sheet

perceudw It certainly is to the credit of a Frenchman to catch so completely the spirit of a thoroughly English scene like this one from " King Henry IV." The salacious and liquor-loving old knight is entertaining Doll Tear-Sheet, a lady of light character, and Dame Quickly, with an account of the misdoings and shortcomings of Prince Hal and his friend Poins, who, disguised as serving-men, glower at him from the doorway on the left. Pipers and fiddlers have been summoned for the old fellow's amusement, and sack is plentiful. Falstaff wears his buckram jerkin and his belt and spurs won by word valor. His jolly, rubicund face is in marked contrast to the white skin of the wheedling woman beside him. The arrangement of light, although slightly divided, is still consistent.

Signed at the right.   Height, 39 inches; width, 61 inches.

VASES AND STATUARY.

143—ONE JAPANESE BRONZE VASE.
  With clear-cut relief ornamentation.
  Height, 31 inches.

144—ONE PEDESTAL.
  Walnut, handsomely carved.
  Height, 42 inches; top, 15 by 11 inches.

145—TWO VASES.
  Old Japanese, lacquer and gold ornamentation.
  Height, 48 inches; diameter, 16 inches.

146—BRONZE VASE.
  Unique design, richly ornamented, with ring handles and removable base.
  Height, 31 inches; width, 15 inches.

147—BRONZE FIGURE.
  Sesostris, one of the Pharaohs, by E. Picault.
  A stately figure of classic lines.
  Height, 28 inches.

148—BRONZE GROUP: "KABYLE SHEPHERD."
  By Waegen. A magnificent and spirited piece, showing the Algerian holding up in triumph the head and skin of a lioness just slain in the rescue of one of the flock. The dogs lie on the carcass. The horse shows strength, spirit, and pride. The easy poise, the loose robe, and the ready grouping account for the great interest this group aroused at the *Beaux Arts* in 1870.
  Height, 48 inches.

  Carved walnut base.
  Height, 36 inches; width, 18 inches.

149—MASSIVE BRONZE GROUP.

J. B. Mather 355.—

By L. Grégoire. Representing Orestes and his sister Electra. Taken from the story told by Æschylus in "The Furies," where Orestes is swearing to avenge the death of his father, Agamemnon, by taking the life of his mother Clytemnestra, who had murdered him. A magnificent bronze, full of force and character.

Height, 42 inches ; width, 22 inches.

Red porphyry pedestal ; highly polished.

Height, 30 inches.

FINE ART BOOKS.

150—AUDSLEY AND BOWLES. "KERAMIC ART OF JAPAN."

With a large number of full-page illustrations. Two volumes, folio, bound in half red morocco. Liverpool, 1865.

151—AUDSLEY (George A.). "THE ORNAMENTAL ARTS OF JAPAN."

In four parts, in five portfolios. Plates in chromolithography and monochrome, with description, in the following divisions : Embroidery, Textile Fabrics, Lacquer, Incrusted Work, Metal Work, Cloisonné.

152—GORRINGE (Henry H., Lieut. - Commander U. S. Navy). "EGYPTIAN OBELISKS."

With 51 full-page illustrations, 32 artotypes, 18 engravings, and 1 chromolithograph; folio in blue cloth binding. Published for the author in New York.

153—Dickinson's "Comprehensive Pictures of the Great Exhibition of 1851."

From the originals painted for H. R. H. Prince Albert, by Messrs. Nash, Hughe, and Roberts, R.A. Royal folio, leather binding.

154—Waring (J. B.) "Masterpieces of Industrial Art and Sculpture at the International Exhibition of 1862."

With a large number of plates, superbly finished in gold, silver, and colors. 3 vols. royal folio, red morocco extra, gilt edges. London, 1863.

An illustrated record of famous specimens of metal work, glass painting, etc.

155—Dumas (F. G.). "Illustrated Biographies of Modern Artists."

With full-page etchings, and numerous illustrations in text. Folio, morocco, Paris, 1882.

The biographies with portraits and plates of important works of the following artists : Leighton, Millais, Herkomer, Alma-Tadema, Baudry, Israels, Menzel, Von Piloty, Makart, Hook, Cabanel, and Meissonier.

156—Mentz (Paul). "Les Chefs-d'œuvre de la peinture Italienne."

Folio, morocco, Paris, 1870.

Ouvrage contenant vingt planches chromolithographique, executées par F. Kellerhoven, trente planches sur bois et quarante culs-de-lampe et lettres ornées.

THE AMERICAN ART ASSOCIATION,

MANAGERS.

THOMAS E. KIRBY,

AUCTIONEER.

www.ingramcontent.com/pod-product-compliance
Lightning Source LLC
Chambersburg PA
CBHW021534270326
41930CB00008B/1253